T0137560

THERE IS A BLACKOUT IN THE CHURCH, AND GOD IS NOT PLEASED

THERE IS A BLACKOUT IN THE CHURCH, AND GOD IS NOT PLEASED

Bishop Edward Charles Gresham

Pastor and Founder of Moving in Christ Outreach Ministries

WESTBOW
PRESS®
A DIVISION OF THOMAS NELSON
& ZONDERVAN

WestBow Press books may be ordered through booksellers or by contacting:

WestBow Press
A Division of Thomas Nelson & Zondervan
1663 Liberty Drive
Bloomington, IN 47403
www.westbowpress.com
1 (866) 928-1240

ISBN: 978-1-5127-0322-1 (sc)
ISBN: 978-1-5127-0323-8 (e)

Library of Congress Control Number: 2015912818

Print information available on the last page.

WestBow Press rev. date: 10/28/2015

To my wife and four sons and all my family and friends

Contents

The Purpose of This Book

Remember—our purpose is to get the true light back on in our lives. To wake up the whole person, body, soul, and spirit, reaching the heart and the mind to save the soul.

For at least the last forty to fifty years, we have seen all kinds of evil spirits and darkness hatched from the pit of hell to replace the truth. We have only one way to be made whole in our spirits, and that is to repent and put our total trust in Jesus Christ. Only He can turn our lights on—or *back* on. In the beginning, God created the heaven and the earth, and the earth was without form and void. Darkness was upon the face of the deep, and the Spirit of God moved upon the face of the waters, and God said, "Let there be light," and there was light (John 1:1–17; Genesis 1). Walk as children of light (Ephesians 5:8).

In these last days, there are a lot of "blackouts" in the church, and God is not pleased. Fathers, mothers, uncles, aunts, sons, daughters, apostles, bishops, elders, pastors, teachers, and this whole nation are under God.

CHAPTER 1

Blackout

A blackout is a temporary loss of consciousness or power, a disconnect from our power source. The church, the body of Christ, is the born-again believers and true worshipers. We are the church, not the steel, nails, mortar, bricks, and wood. Blackouts happen all the time in the secular world, but they should not happen all the time or every day in the body of Christ.

The Bible tells us to pray that we enter not into temptation (Matthew 6:13, 26:41; 2 Peter 2:9). Yes, there is a lot of junk to get into. That's why we need to trust and rely on him, Jesus Christ. "Trust in the Lord with all thine Heart, and lean not unto thine own understanding. In all thy ways acknowledge Him and He shall direct thy paths" (Proverbs 3:5–6 KJV).

Listen—sin separates us from the Lord. Many messes have cut off our power: pornography, lies, bad relationships, and abuse, mental and physical. Generational things pass down to you that do not have anything to do with the Lord: Masons, Eastern Stars, Frat brothers and sisters, Shriners, and all these secret clubs. And homosexuality too is taking over a lot of our states. Legislators are passing laws that go against the Word of God.

Talk about being seduced—we are naked with all our clothes off. There is no Spirit of God anywhere.

The Lord gave me this message to preach in 1999: there is a blackout in the church, and God is not pleased. We are in everything but the Holy Ghost. Read Matthew 10:26–28. The Lord is sending a warning to you today. "If my people which are called by my name, shall humble themselves, and pray, and seek my face, and turn from their wicked ways, then I will Hear from Heaven and will forgive their sins, and will Heal their land" (2 Chronicles 7:14 KJV).

Simply put, our land needs a healing, from the pulpit to the lay members. "There is a way which seemeth right unto a man, but the end thereof is the ways of death" (Proverbs 14:12–16:25). Things we know and things we do not know can hurt or kill us. We must guard our hearts, minds, and spirits from bad foods. Our natural bodies need good food to live on. What about the spiritual person? It needs lots of prayer and fasting, and always it needs the Word of God—the written Word as well as the spoken word. There's no other way around it.

CHAPTER 2

The Church

The church is not the brick and mortar, the steel or wood frame, but the New Testament. The church is a group of born-again people, not a man-made building. The word *church* comes from the Greek word *ekklesia*, meaning "the called out." The word originally signified a group of people assembled for a civil purpose (see Acts 19:32). Where the Word of God is rendered *assembly*, it is used to denote the body of the faithful in Christ Jesus. The church universal includes all those who have believed and obeyed the gospel. "Praising God and having favor with all the people, and the Lord added to the church daily such as should be saved" (Acts 2:47 KJV).

> Husbands, love your wives even as Christ loved the church and gave Himself for it, that He might sanctify and cleanse it with the washing of water by the Word, that He might present it to Himself a glorious church not having spot or wrinkle, or any such thing: but that it should be Holy and without blemish. (Ephesians 5:25–27)

Take heed therefore unto yourselves and to all the flock, over which the Holy Ghost hath made you overseers, to feed the church of God, which He hath purchased with His own blood. (Acts 20:28)

The church is also called the spiritual body of Christ. "And hath put all things under His feet and gave Him to be head over all things to the church, which is His body, the fullness of Him that filleth all in all" (Ephesians 1:22–23 KJV).

And He is the Head of the body. The church: who is the beginning, the first born from the dead: that in all things that He might have the preeminence, for it pleased the father that in Him should all fullness dwell.

And having made peace through the blood of His cross, by Him to reconcile all things unto Himself: by Him, I say, whether they are things on earth, or things in Heaven. And you that were sometimes alienated and enemies in your mind by wicked works yet now hath He reconciled.

In the body of His flesh through death, to present you Holy and unblamable and unreprovable in His sight, if ye continue in faith grounded and settled and be not moved away from the hope of the gospel, which ye have Heard, and which was preached to every creature which is under Heaven: where of I Paul am made a minister:

who now rejoice in my sufferings for you and fill up that which is behind of affections of Christ in my flesh for His body's sake, which is the church: whereof I am made a minister according to the dispensation of God which is given to me for you to fulfill the Word of God: even the mystery which hath been hid from ages and from generations, but now is made manifest (made known) to His saints: To whom God would make known what is the riches of the glory of His mystery among the gentiles: which is Christ in you, the hope of glory.

Whom we preach, warning every man, and teaching every man in all wisdom: that we may present every man perfect in Christ Jesus: where unto I also labor, striving according to His working, which worketh in me mightily. (Colossians 1:18–19 & Colossians 2:9-10 KJV)

And that from a child thou hast known the Holy scriptures, which are able to make thee wise unto salvation through faith which is in Christ Jesus. (2 Timothy 3:15)

And I John saw the Holy city, new Je-ru'sa-lem, coming down from God out of Heaven, prepared as a bride adorned for Her husband. (Revelation 21:2)

The church shows God's eternal wisdom, "to the intent that now unto the principalities and powers in Heavenly places might be known by the church the manifold wisdom of God," prophesied by Christ (Ephesians 3:10). "And I say also unto thee, that thou art Peter and upon this rock I will build my church: and the gates of Hell shall not prevail against it" (Matthew 16:18). Jesus is the Rock, and everything else is sinking sand.

The church was established on Pentecost (Acts 2). In the New Testament, the city name is used to designate a local congregation of born-again believers: "Unto the church of God which is at Corinth, to them that are sanctified in Christ Jesus, called to be saints, with all that in every place call upon the name of Jesus Christ our Lord, both theirs and ours" (1 Corinthians 1:2).

In this geographical sense of the word, it is often used in the plural: "churches." "Salute one another with a Holy kiss. The churches of Christ salute you" (Romans 16:16 KJV). "And all brethren which are with me, unto the churches of Ga-la'-tia" (Galatians 1:2). "John to the seven churches which are in Asia: glory be unto you, and peace, from Him which is, and which was and which is to come, and from the seven spirits which are before His throne" (Revelation 1:4).

CHAPTER 3

Why the Church?

Let's start by looking at the words of Matthew: "And from the days of John the Baptist until now, the kingdom of Heaven suffereth, violence. And the violent take it by force" (Matthew 11:12 KJV). Jesus Christ, our Lord and Savior, has already done the work, but we have to live totally in Him to have victory from ruin.

"Therefore rejoice, ye Heavens, and ye that dwell in them. Woe to the inhabiters of the earth and of the sea: for the devil is come down unto you, having great wrath, because He knoweth that He hath but a short time" (Revelation 12:12 KJV). The blackout has the church in darkness, with the loss of consciousness and power. The Lord wants us to die to sin and flesh but live and stand in the truth in these evil times.

> This know also, that in the last days, perilous times shall come, these evil times, for men shall be lovers of their own selves, covetous, boasters, proud, blasphemers, disobedient to parents, unthankful, unholy, without natural affection, trucebreakers, false accusers, incontinent, fierce,

> despisers of those that are good, traitors, Heady, high-minded, lovers of pleasures more than lovers of God, having a form of Godliness, but denying thy power thereof: from such turn away. (2 Timothy 3:1–5)

We better separate ourselves from people who do not allow the Lord's power to work in their lives.

> Having a form of Godliness, even the people that pretend. For of this sort are they which creep into houses, and lead captives silly women laden with sins, led away with diver's lust. Ever learning and never able to come to the knowledge of the truth. (2 Timothy 3:6–7)

We have church folks who live a lie, or shall we say lies. Sinners laugh or say, "That's why I don't go to church—nobody is right." Some may be playing games, but Jesus Christ has real, genuine, born-again saints who have come out. Please do not use that for a cop-out. All unrighteousness is sin, and "the wages of sin is death" (Romans 6:23 KJV).

The Devil tried to get Jesus Christ himself to come down from truth to falsehood or wrongdoing.

> Then was Jesus led up of the spirit into the wilderness to be tempted of the devil, and fasted forty days and forty nights, He was afterwards hungered. And when the temper came to Him, He said, if thou be the son of God, command that these stones be made bread. But He answered

and said, it is written, "Man shall not live by bread alone, but by every Word that proceedeth out of the mouth of God" then the devil taketh Him up into the Holy city, and setteth Him on a pinnacle of the temple, and said unto Him, if thou be the Son of God, cast thyself down: for it is written, He shall give His angels charge concerning thee: and in their hands they shall bear thee up, lest at any time thou dash thy foot against a stone. Jesus said unto Him, It is written again, thou shall not attempt the Lord thy God." Again the devil taketh Him up into an exceeding high mountain, and sheweth Him all the kingdoms of the world, and the glory of them: and saith unto Him, all these things will I give thee, if thou wilt fall down and worship me. Then saith Jesus unto him, "Get thee hence Satan: for it is written, thou shall worship the Lord thy God, and Him only shalt thou serve." (Matthew 4:1–10)

The Lord used Himself, His Word. "In the beginning was the Word, and the Word was with God, and the word was god. the same was in the beginning with god. All things were made by Him: and without Him was not anything made that was made. In Him was life: and the life was the light of men, and the light shineth in darkness: and the darkness comprehended it not" (John 1:1–5).

Our problem in this whole nation is that we have ignorantly abandoned our spiritual persons for the cares of this world. Our Lord and Savior came out on top every time. We can't just quote Scripture; like Jesus Christ, we have to live it daily.

The gospel of John says, "The thief cometh not, but for to steal, and to kill, and to destroy." He wants to take you out. But Jesus said, "I am come that they might have life and that they might have it more abundantly" (John 10:10). Live life in the fullness of Jesus Christ.

The Devil wins when we lie or cheat; when we do drugs, pop pills, or drink alcohol; when we rape women or molest our young boys and girls; when we beat up on our women and kill each other. All races need to come back to Jesus Christ. If you wonder why our kids are in the streets, living like villains, robbing and killing, joining gangs, then look to their homes. Their homes are broken. Men are not being fathers. Women are not being mothers. Children get no home training. Grandfathers and grandmothers are robbing the cradles. Mothers are on crack cocaine and selling themselves just to have a pair of pants and a drunk in the house. The jails are overrun with our young men and women.

Yes, it is your money, but think. We spend billions of dollars on dogs and cats for hip replacements and other medical treatment. But we will not raise a hand to help human beings.

Something is sadly wrong in our society. We need to start loving one another. There will only be one heaven and one hell for blacks and whites and all the other races too. We need to love more. Out of my love for people and love for God, I write to you today. God is not pleased.

Men, you don't have to play make-believe. You were made in the image of God (Genesis 1:24, 2:18). Then God made woman for the man. Not man for man or woman for woman; that is out of order. "God is not the author of confusion, but of peace, as in all churches of the saints" (1 Corinthians 14:33). Confusion is a spirit of error.

Strip clubs, adult stores, inventors of evil things—these break down homes and family relationships. The word on the street is it's better to shack up than to marry. But Paul tells us, "If they cannot contain, let them marry: for it is better to marry than to burn" (1 Corinthians 7:9). Burn in the flesh, but please make sure you plan for marriage and get marriage counseling. Planning for and finding the right person is a lot better than just jumping into something.

Men and women, pray and seek the Lord. Women, the Lord never told you to go looking for men. I know that's old fashioned, but that's what's messing us up—not seeking the Lord about our relationships. I know we think we can change other people, but the truth is you cannot even change yourself. It takes the Lord to do it. So submit to His ways.

"Who so findeth a wife findeth a good thing, and obtaineth favor of the Lord" (Proverbs 18:22). One man, one woman: this pleases the Lord.

Our children are getting into gangs: Bloods, Crips, Latin Kings, Gangster Disciples, Vice Lords, Hell's Angels, and Satan's Disciples, just to name a few. There are hundreds more. Why? These things are of the world. Join God's club.

"Now when they heard this, they were pricked in their heart and said unto Peter and to the rest of the apostles, Men and brethren, what shall we do? Then Peter said unto them, repent and be baptized every one of you in the name of Jesus Christ for the remission of sins, and ye shall receive the gift of the Holy Ghost" (Acts 2:37–38). The bottom line is the Devil wants to cheat you out of your true blessing: living in heaven forever.

CHAPTER 4

God Is Not Pleased

The Bible is very clear about what is pleasing to God and what is not. Let's start by looking at Genesis:

> And the Lord God called unto Adam, and said unto Him. Where art thou?

> And He said, "I heard thy voice in the garden, and I was afraid, because I was naked: and I hid myself." And He said who told thee that thou wast naked? Have thou eaten off the tree. Whereof I commanded thee that thou shouldest not eat? And the man said the woman thou gavest to be with me, she gave me of the tree, and I did eat. And the Lord God said unto the woman. What is this that thou hast done? and the woman said the serpent beguiled me, and I did eat.

> And the Lord God said unto the serpent, because thou hast done this, thou art cursed above all

cattle, and above every beast of the field: Upon thy belly shall thou go and dust shalt thou eat all the days of thy life: And I will put enmity between thee and the woman, and between thy seed and her seed: it shall bruise thy head, and thou shall bruise his heel. Unto the woman He said, I will greatly multiply thy sorrow and thy conception: in sorrow thou shalt forth bring children: and thy desire shall be thy husband, and he shall rule over thee. And unto Adam He said, because thou hast harkened unto the voice of thy wife, and hast eaten of the tree, of which I commanded thee saying thou shall not eat of it: cursed is the ground for thy sake: in sorrow shalt thou eat of it all the days of thy life: thorns also and thistles shall it bring forth to thee: and thou shalt eat the herb of the field: in the sweat of thy face shalt thou eat bread, till thou return unto the ground: for out of it wast thou taken: for dust thou art, and unto dust shalt thou return. (3:9–19)

This does not sound like the Lord was pleased with them. All involved were cursed for being disobedient.

Living in ways that are unrighteous, evil, and wicked is never pleasing to God. Obedience to the voices of evil people always comes from the Father of Lies, that old serpent, the Devil. "But I fear lest by any means, as the serpent beguiled eve through His subtlety so your minds should be corrupted from the simplicity that is in Christ" (2 Corinthians 11:3).

The Lord has always wanted humankind to please him. "Let us Hear the conclusion of the whole matter: fear God and keep His commandments for this is the whole duty of man" (Ecclesiastes

12:13). Sin has always brought humankind down because it does not please the Lord. "And God saw that the wickedness of man was great in the earth, and that every imagination of the thoughts of His heart was only evil continually. And it repented the Lord that He had made man on the earth, and it grieved Him at His Heart" (Genesis 6:5–6). This does not sound like the Lord was happy or excited about humankind. Nor was the Lord pleased with this: "The earth was also corrupt before God, and the earth was filled with violence. And God looked upon the earth, and behold it was corrupt: for all flesh had corrupted His way upon the earth" (Genesis 6:11–12).

That was thousands of years ago, but take a look at our universe today: violence, crime, hatred, killing, stealing, living like animals, racism, discrimination, modern-day slavery. It's a different day, but the same games are going on. We all need to take a good look in the mirror at what we can do to stand up in righteousness. Adults, young people, fathers, mothers, grandparents, sons, daughters, sisters, brothers, apostles, bishops, elders, evangelists, deacons, pastors, and teachers—we all need to take a stand now. Do not compromise the Word of God.

This is what happened in Lot's day: "Then the Lord rained upon Sodom and upon Gomo'rah brimstone and fire from the Lord out of Heaven: and He overthrew those cities, and all the plain, and all the inhabitants of the cities, and that which grew upon the ground" (Genesis 19:24–25). Look at some of the things the inhabitants did, especially the sins committed with their bodies against the commandments of God: homosexuality, incest, drunkenness. They showed no respect for each other.

It's the same or worse today. We need revival for our yokes to be destroyed.

> For the wrath of God is revealed from Heaven
> against all ungodliness and unrighteousness of
> men, who hold the truth in unrighteousness ...
> Because that, when they knew God, neither were
> thankful, but became vain in their imaginations
> and their foolish Heart was darkened. Professing
> themselves to be wise, they became fools and
> change the glory of the incorruptible God into
> an image made like to corruptible man, and
> to birds and four-footed beasts and creeping
> things. Wherefore God also gave them up to
> uncleanness through the lust of their own
> Hearts, to dishonor their own bodies between
> themselves: Who changed the truth of God into
> a lie and worshipped and serve the creature more
> than the creator, who is blessed forever. Amen.

> For this cause God gave them up unto vile
> affections. (Romans 1:18, 21–26)

Affection in the right mind-set is a feeling of love. Real love is
not false; it's genuine. The love of God is always pure and clean.

> For even their women did change the natural use
> into that which is against nature: and likewise
> also the men, leaving the natural use of the
> women, burned in their lust one toward another:
> men with men working that which is unseemly,
> and receiving in themselves that recompense of
> their error which was meet. and even as they did
> not like to certain God in their knowledge, God
> gave them over to a reprobate mind to do the

things which are not convenient: being filled with all unrighteousness, fornication, wickedness, covetousness, maliciousness, full of envy, murder, debate, deceit, malignity,, whisperers, backbiters, haters of God. Despiteful, proud, boasters, inventors of evil things, disobedient to parents.

Without understanding, covenant breakers, without natural affection, implacable, unmerciful: who knowing the judgment of God that they which commit such things are worthy of death, not only do the same, but have pleasure in them that do them. (Romans 1:26–32)

God is not pleased. We need to love the person but not the sin. Let's get the light back on here in the United States of America. Sin is what has broken down our country. "Righteousness exalted a nation: but sin is a reproach to any people (Proverbs 14:34). What has happened to our biblical principles? We have left our first love, Jesus Christ.

Preachers, stop compromising the Word. Hell is not worth it. Wake up! Cry aloud! Repent, be baptized, and be filled with the Holy Ghost before it's too late. God is not pleased.

CHAPTER 5

Everything Is Not God

Leaders are the ones who have influence over the Lord's flock. "But take Heed lest by any means this liberty of yours become a stumbling block to them that are weak" (1 Corinthians 8:9). Leaders are so caught up with getting everyone to agree with them, or to rock the boat to make sure the money doesn't stop, that they teach another gospel. The true gospel of Jesus Christ will free us from the bondage of sin and death. Going along with everything the world is doing does not line up with the Word of God. Let's cry to God that He sends revivals to the whole body of Christ.

Preachers, hear the voice of God: "The fruit of the righteous is a tree of life; and he that winneth souls is wise" (Proverbs 11:30). False prophets are doomed. If it's not of the Lord, it is of the Devil. Dare to be different. Stop going along with lies.

Will the real people of God please stand up? As men and women of God, let's put some heat on our elected officials. They are stealing, cheating, lying, and taking advantage of others. This blackout covers all of us.

Passing ungodly laws and looking for a great outcome is not

good for our nation. "If my people which are called by my name will humble themselves pray and seek my face and turn from their wicked ways: then will I hear from heaven and will forgive their sin and will heal their land" (2 Chronicles 7:14).

In modern-day slavery, banks give credit cards with high interest rates, which take twenty to thirty years to pay off. If you don't have the cash, think about waiting. We are not thinking ahead. We end up with jacked-up credit and for years can't even get a loan.

Take a good look around. It's not just the credit score. There are no jobs. Open your eyes. You're showing your underwear, your big T-shirts. Open your eyes. Gangs are taking over some communities. Open your eyes. Young people are shacked up, having babies like rabbits. Open your eyes. Young people are refusing to grow up. Open your eyes.

Radio, talk-show hosts, TV shows, and social media are teaching a lot of mess. They're thugs with the wrong mind-set. Parents, we need to take a good look in the mirror. Men are not teaching their sons. Women are not teaching their daughters. There is a big breakdown in some of our homes.

This is the world view: jump from man to man, from woman to woman, or from man to woman. Can't see eye to eye? Get rid of him. Get another one. Wake up! That's the wrong mind-set. This is not TV. Wake up!

Everything is not God. This is why we need the Word of God to take root in our lives. Our lives, our minds need to change, and this change can only come in Jesus Christ. Joining some club will not do it.

CHAPTER 6

Eyes on the System

Watch the banking system. One thing we know: in these last days, our money, our method, and our credit have already changed in this country. The pay that most of us are making has not changed in fifteen to twenty years. House prices have gone up, but not our pay. Gas prices have gone through the roof, but not our pay. Food and clothing prices have skyrocketed, but not our pay.

Most of our jobs over the last fifteen years have gone overseas. Some of the same congresspeople who voted our jobs away are now playing the blame game. The United States owes other countries. People from other countries have always been able to come here and get a seven-year tax break. We were not afforded the same in other countries. Now we wonder about the mess we are in here in the United States.

Keep watching. The new world order is next. Everything is already in place. If you don't have good credit, you will not be able to buy or sell. Everything is about your credit score. People who say they don't like to eat certain things or cannot wear certain things keep getting hoodwinked. It's time for all of us to wake up and open our eyes. You can use a bank for years, know everyone from the branch manager to the teller, and you still cannot qualify for a loan. What about your character? It does not matter. It's your credit score.

People ask me all the time, "What is this world coming to?" and I reply, "The end."

Just fifteen years ago, everybody was running, wondering if the world would end. Two weeks into January 2000, everybody went back to the same life: living without God, treating one another wrongly, telling lies, cheating, and killing. It's all about greedy, arrogant, self-centered *me*. We need to turn back to God.

They are just waiting to bring in this one world government, one world religion, and one world currency. Medvedev, the former Russian president, showed off a sample coin of the new world currency at the G-8 summit meeting on June 10, 2009. It said "Unity in Diversity" on the front. All this stuff is in place; they are just waiting to present it to the world. Waiting on the right moment. The way things in the United States are going, it will be very soon. Wake up, and wake up now.

Keep watching the news. All of this is staged, so you will see and hear what they want you to see and hear. Start praying for revivals to break out all over the United States.

It's not just Republicans or Democrats. Both parties lie to get elected. All of these men and women are in secret clubs. They join by false oaths. "And let none of you imagine evil in your hearts against his neighbor: and love no false oath: for all these are thing that I hate, saith the Lord" (Zachariah 8:17). Gangs are the same. Adults and kids love their little clubs. Both are wrong. They're covering up wrongdoing—hurting and killing others just get theirs. We all need to wake up.

Pastors, stop compromising with evil. The outcome will always be evil. When will it stop? This one thing has already weakened our nation. Wake up.

CHAPTER 7

It's Not Free

For years, people have been thinking, "It's free." Well, it's not free. These services will soon be over. No insurance, no medical care. No longer will the hospital wait on you without insurance. Government cards will soon be cut off. It's not free. We all had better learn to live within our means. Before it's over, everyone will know not to put trust in humankind. The Word of God is clear. "It is better to trust in the Lord than to put confidence in man, it is better to trust in the Lord than to put confidence in princes" (Psalm 118:8–9).

People are always looking for something free. Nothing's free. You may get it free, but someone paid a price for it. We have the best accountants and bookkeepers, yet just about every city in the United States is $10 or $20 million in the hole. It's not free. Taxpayers paid into the system. How can these accountants make these mistakes year after year?

The lottery games, we are told, provide funds for the schools, yet they close the schools down. What happened to the money? It's not free. Someone paid into that lie.

Insurance companies get billions of dollars a year. People pay their premiums for years and never file a claim. Then a storm hits, and the insurance companies cry broke to get out of paying. Who foots the bill? The taxpayers. We lose our jobs, our homes, and everything we have worked for. We start over. What happens to our payoff? It's not free. Someone had to pay.

There's no free lunch. The bling-bling will soon be over. It's not free.

Young girls, please wake up. Stop giving yourself away to a pair of pants. If you can get the milk free, then why buy the cow? It's not free.

Some say, "I'll get it and kill it." Just look at the mind-set. One day we will pay for the wrong things we do.

We get our produce from all around the world. Meantime, a lot of our farmers agree with the government not to grow crops—corn, soy beans, and other crops. It's not free. Learn how to grow different crops before it's over. We may be forced to do it all over again. It's not free.

People you look down your nose at may have to help you out. There's so much going on. We are so occupied with all these gadgets, we are blinded. The Devil has a lot of his mess already set up.

Many prophets have spoken God's Word concerning these things. Woe be unto any nation or people that does not heed the Lord's voice. "Thus saith the Lord of hosts. the God of Israel: behold, I will bring upon this city and upon all her towns all the evil that I have pronounced against it, because they have hardened their necks, that they might not hear my words" (Jeremiah 19:15).

It's not free. The price is our souls. Jesus paid for you and me with His blood, and you are willing to give it to the Devil for free. Think about it.

Chapter 8

Take Back Your Dedication

First of all, dedication is consecration, a setting aside for a purpose. That purpose it to totally give yourself, to clear out all the blockage—I mean everything that hinders your purpose of receiving strength, insight, and power from the Lord. Clear your very being, your body, soul, and spirit, to receive only from Jesus Christ. Shut out everything else.

Please release people who you feel wronged you. Run the Devil off your battlefield, which is in your mind. Get the mess out— all of it. In order to be free, you have to free others. It does not matter what you think they did. If you caused the error, ask for forgiveness.

You want this to be a spiritual overdose in the Holy Ghost, so the Lord can overpower you when you come out. You want everyone to know that you have been with the Lord—not for show, but with power. Apostles, preachers, bishops, elders, evangelists: all these walls will fall. You can't live every day in the flesh and think you can have this power. Gifts are given without repentance, but for that genuine anointing, we need to bear our crosses.

I know already that Jesus has borne His cross. Yes, He did, and He is not on it any longer. He's at the right hand of the throne of God.

"How be it this kind goeth not out but by prayer, and fasting" (Matthew 17:21). The best way is to set yourself aside, not get into everything going on. That's one way to miss our visitation from the Lord.

From time to time, people say, "The Lord's not healing like in Bible days." Well, we are still living in Bible days. Many just don't believe and have the faith that God still heals, the faith that God still can cast the Devil out, the faith that God still works miracles. If your god has stopped, try mine. He still heals. He still cast out devils. He still works miracles.

The Enemy tried to run a friend of mine out of his house. There was a spirit in the kitchen and dining room area. He invited my wife and I down for prayer. We prayed, and the Lord cast those tormenting spirits out. The Lord gave peace.

Some have allowed the adversary to slay them with his lies. The thief cometh not but to steal and kill and destroy. The good news is that Jesus said, "I am come that they might have life and that they might have it more abundantly" (John 10:10). Jesus Christ always has you and me in mind, but we have to seek Him with our whole hearts. We have to put faith, total confidence, and trust in Him.

All through the gospels, Jesus showed His disciples how to obtain this power and keep it. Some look for it in the wrong places. They look for it in material things: in people, in money, in a can of beer or a liquor bottle, or in the wrong kind of sex. Yes, sex outside of marriage is wrong. Start seeking the Lord.

Ask Him for the spirit of prayer and fasting to take away all these evil addictions.

In order to do the work of Jesus Christ, prayer and fasting are the only way. Spend that quiet time with the Lord. "But seek ye first the kingdom of God, and his righteousness: and all these things shall be added unto you" (Matthew 6:33). We all need to seek the Lord's will for our lives.

One thing is for sure: everyone has an opinion. Godly men and women hold to God's principles. The Word of God is what we all need to live and submit to. To live in the flesh is death, but to live in the Spirit is life.

It's human nature to seek the stuff first. That's the thing about the Devil: he shows you the stuff to entangle you. He always shows us the things that take us out of the plan of God. He always makes junk or wrongdoing appealing to the flesh. The Lord can say to us, "Get up and pray." We get up and find something to eat. We get up and turn the TV on. In the end, we do not obey the Lord.

That is why we need to be taught the Word of God the proper way. That is why you need a church home—to make sure you get the Bible study and learn what the Bible says. "Forsake not the assembly of ourselves together" (Hebrews 10:25). There is a blessing among our sisters and brothers in the Lord, coming together to learn, encourage, and strengthen each other in ways you just cannot do alone. Even if you have been in the Lord for a while, sometimes we still need each other. You know, in the world we had or hung out with our posse. But in the Lord, it's better than anything you ever could do in the world.

The Enemy wants you to think otherwise. The Enemy wants to come and slay you and me.

Guard your heart and soul; refuse to go out like that. Jesus Christ has already made it possible for you to do it. All of us need to seek His truths in order to live in them. That's why we need pastors to feed the flock of God.

And we better run away from all who do not preach the whole Bible and who are not filled with the Holy Ghost. If the Lord is not using you, then the Devil will. We need to know the difference. There is a bunch of lies out there; that's why we need to study to know and understand what the Word of God says. If you seek Him, He can and will show you what's right. He came to cleanse us from all unrighteousness, to make us complete in Him.

CHAPTER 9

A Little about the Dead Man

I was a sinner, a man who did not have the Lord in his life. I was a man living without God, His wisdom, and His knowledge. I was blind. I was the walking dead: going to the church building but still dead; singing in the choir but still dead; helping others from time to time but still dead. I was in the mess, and the way I lived was by misusing the Lord's temple, His body.

Oh, I was pretty good in my own thinking: cheating, telling lies, on my way to the Devil Hell. I went to church on Sunday morning and could not wait to get home to pop my Miller High Life. I could not wait to go hang out with the boys and, you know, find some girls to get into something. I was still dead.

But one Sunday morning, my sister invited me to go to a little church called Pure Church of Jesus Christ. The pastor was Elder Charles Davis. The Lord was really using this man of God to lay hands on the sick. He just pointed to some, and the Lord touched them. Well, I'd never seen it anything like it.

CHAPTER 10

A Little about the Man
Who Came Alive

Elder Charles Davis would tell people to lift up their hands, and before he touched them, they would hit the floor. I was amazed at what was happening.

At the end of the service, they said, "This is Sister Doris's brother."

He said, "Son, can I pray for you?"

I said, "Well, sure."

I walked out into the aisle. Elder Davis came down and laid his hands on me. I began to feel the Spirit of God go through my body. He prayed and spoke a word from the Lord to me: "Son, your life after today will not be the same."

I tell you, after hearing and seeing that, I wanted more. I started going to Bible study and Sunday school midweek revivals. The Lord had started to change my life—but I had to admit that I was a sinner. In order for Jesus Christ to save you, you have to admit that you are a sinner. I repented of all my sins and was baptized in the name of Jesus Christ. I was taught the Word of God.

I learned that the Lord loved me and gave himself for me. He died and rose again on the third day to redeem humankind. Jesus Christ is the only way to have eternal life. I found out so many things in the Word of God that, for all the years I'd been going to church, I had never known. But I had to go to Bible study, had to go to church services. Friday night, Saturday, Sunday morning, Sunday night—some say that's too much church, but I say it's not enough.

You see, the Enemy does not take a day off. We always need to keep our guards up. To do that, we have to put on the whole armor of God.

> Put on the whole armor of God, that ye may be able to stand against the wiles of the devil; for we wrestle not against flesh and blood, but against principalities, against powers, against the rulers of darkness of this world, against spiritual wickedness in high places.

> wherefore take unto you the whole armor of God, that ye may be able to withstand in the evil day, and having done all, to stand, stand therefore, having your loins girt about the truth, and having on the breastplate of righteousness: and your feet shod with preparation of the gospel of peace: above all, taking the shield of faith, where with ye shall be able to quench all the fiery darts of the wicked, and take the helmet of salvation, and

the sword of the spirit, which is the word of God:
praying always with all prayer and supplication
in the spirit, and watching there unto with all
perseverance and supplication for all saints; and
for me, that utterance may be given unto me, that
I may open my mouth boldly, to make known the
mystery of the gospel. (Ephesians 6:11–19)

If we as preachers do not preach the word of God, people will think it's okay to keep on doing wrong.

Women, men, some of you have been molested by stepdads, uncles, aunts, sisters, brothers—people that you trusted who let you down. But Jesus Christ did not let you down. Women, there are still some good men out there. Men, there are still some good women out there. Men turning to men or women turning women as spouses is out of order. Even if they pass these damnable laws, animals should not be smarter than human beings. I have never seen a horse and a cow mate. I have never seen dog and a cat mate. The bull chases after the heifer.

Men, lose all effeminate, womanish ways: hippie, dreadlocks, slick, Jheri curls, tattoos, little earbobs, and dresses. Women, you are trying to be hard. It does not matter how much you work out, put on those dirty boy jeans, cut your hair off, or whisper in the ear of another woman. Lay or play, you are still a woman, and every month the system of God is still at work.

God made man, and then He made woman. Just for the record, *God doesn't make mistakes.* That is a lie and a trick of the Devil. The Lord still loves you, but not your sins. *All unrighteousness is sin.*

repent ye therefore, and be converted, that your sins may be blotted out, when the times of refreshing shall come from the presence of the lord.

And he shall send Je'sus Christ, which before was preached unto you: whom the heaven must receive until the times of restitution of all things, which God hath spoken by the mouth of all his holy prophets since the world began. Come on out while there is still time Repent of your Sins today tomorrow may not be yours the day you hear my voice harden not your heart. (Acts 3:19–21)

CHAPTER 11

Judgment in the House

Judgment is discernment, understanding, intelligence; it can also mean a verdict of a court or a sentence. "For the time is come that judgment must begin at the house of God: and if first begin at us, what shall the end of them that obey not the gospel of God? And if the righteous scarcely be saved, where shall the ungodly and the sinner appear? Wherefore let them that suffer according to the will of God commit the keeping of their souls to him in well doing, as unto the faithful creator" (1 Peter 4:17–19 KIV).

People of God, it is vital that we have a clear understanding of what's really going on in the United States of America, what's happening in your local church, in the body of Christ. Look at everything. This is also a true test for all who name the name of Jesus Christ and for all who wish to depart from evil. The Lord always sends warning, but everyone does not always take heed.

If the righteous are scarcely saved, if they barely make it, then the sinner who does not repent is already damned. That's why it's not how we start but how we finish. Some start running and fight well. Then, somewhere along the way, they slow down and stop fighting.

The Word of God is clear in telling the truth about the judgment of God. In a basketball or football game, all four quarters are important. In a race, it's important to know the route of travel and your stamina. We need a lot of doing right and staying power with the truth in the Word of God in order to finish our course. "Ye did run well: who did hinder you that ye should not obey the truth? This persuasion cometh not of Him that calleth you" (Galatians 5:7–8).

The Lord always wants you and me to stay focused. In the Old Testament, Adam and Eve lost focus and were kicked out of the garden of Eden. King Saul lost his kingdom for disobedience. A prophet was slain by a lion for being disobedient. You can't listen to anybody else when you know that the Lord has spoken to you on a matter.

Judgment can come in many ways. That's why your relationship with God is so important. Study the word of God. Fast and pray. Learn to walk by faith. Live and trust in the Word of God. Don't take in lies. Judgment is in the house. Kings have been taken down because of wickedness. People of low degree have been elevated for living right. It is not popular, but it's pleasing to the Lord.

Look at the signs of the times. Winter is not winter anymore; summer is not summer anymore. It is the last days.

We pray that the Lord helps the whole body of Christ to wake up. Never go along with lies or wrongdoing. "Woe unto them that call evil good, and good evils; that put darkness for light, and light for darkness; bitter for sweet, and sweet for bitter!" (Isaiah 5:20). "Because with lies ye have made the heart of the righteous sad, whom I have not made sad: and strengthened the hand of the wicked, that he should not return from his wicked way, by promising him life" (Ezekiel 13:22). If you keep playing make-believe, these lies will continue to wax worse and worse.

We need a Holy Ghost revival in this land, and we need it now, when we agree with homosexuality, same-sex marriage, and false prophets committing spiritual homicide on our young boy and girls. Just look at this darkness for light. "For the wages for sin is death" (Romans 6:23).

We all have a choice. You choose. We are being warned that the party is over. Judgment is in the house.

CHAPTER 12

The Ladies in the Dark

In every city, large or small around the world, there are ladies so lovely, who so want to be loved, who are so unwise as to allow the darkness of this world to blind their minds with the lust of the cunning hunk.

The hunk is a boy in a man's body. You crave him with all your might, only to learn it's all a lie. His smooth talk and his corrupt mind tie you in a fantasy. You dare to be different, so you run headfirst, all in. No one can talk you down. Everyone is the enemy; everybody is wrong. No one knows. They are blind in your eyes. They don't understand.

They can see your naked, fading beauty. Your mind tells you they are just hating. No. It's you; it's you. "My hunk loves me. He understands." Then one, two, three, four years have passed. You say, "My man will marry me." Six, seven, eight, ten years pass.

Your lying hunk says, "Well, baby, we are common-law married. What's the problem?"

And you say, "Baby, this is not a real marriage in God's eyes."

Twelve years have passed. Your health is fading. You are in and out of the hospital. Your mother, your sister, and your brother plead with you to come to church, to pray, to seek the Lord.

Your hunk tells you another lie. Then it comes out that he has three outside children. The times he said he was working, he was with Cindy, Bessie, Sue—and Jerome. Then he tells you he doesn't want you anymore: you are sick all the time, you are too big, you never please him anymore, and you are ugly. He's going to move out.

On top of all this drama, you start to push your children away. You blame them. They are the reason your lying hunk left you.

Ladies, wake up. Come out of the dark. Mothers are killing their own babies to please their lying hunks. They're changing their core beliefs to live a lie. They're taking pills, crack cocaine, hash, and so on.

And this is not only in small towns or just among blacks. In high places, among whites, Asians, and Mexicans, it's happening. It affects all races and all places, in the United States and around the world. Marriage is a dirty word; shacking up is the going thing. Drugs, sex, and alcohol are the norm. When a person is in darkness, he or she thinks it is the right way.

Ladies, wake up. Repent. Come back to Jesus Christ. He loves you. He will not lie to you or cheat you. Young ladies, Jesus Christ's love is pure.

There is a blackout in the church, and the Lord is not pleased. Raping, sexing, drinking, partying, killing, and being silly and unwise are not good. Women, your lying hunks not only put your lights out. The children think this is the right way. Girls repeat your pattern, Mother. The boy follows the daddy, and sometimes he also takes on the ways of his mother. History will always repeat itself. "As it was in the days of Noah so shall it be in the days of the son of man" (Luke 17:26).

This woman, she never married. She gave all her best years to a liar. Her youth, her strength, and all her beauty were taken by a liar and his tricks. When Sue found out the whole deal about Mr. Kill-Roy, she found the city and location where he lived. He continued to lie and cheat Sue.

Sue was riding by one day and happened to spot his car, so she followed. Another man was driving Kill-Roy's car to pick him up from work. Sue watched in amazement as Kill-Roy came out to get in the car, all happy and full of joy, and gave the dude a big kiss.

Sue could not believe what she was seeing. Bad thoughts went through her mind: "All the money. All the lies. All my best years." So she opened the door of her car and got out, mad, crying big tears that ran down her face.

Kill-Roy happened to look up. "Let's go. That's Sue, okay?" But the crosswalk was blocked with other workers.

Sue was almost to Kill-Roy's car door. Two ministers, a husband-and-wife team, were walking past. They observed her crying and said, "Miss? Miss, can we help? Are you all right? Did these men hurt you? Can we help? Can we pray with you? Can we pray?"

In that moment, Sue broke down. The man and woman of God grabbed her by the hand and prayed. Tears rolled down Sue's face as they prayed for the Lord to touch her and give her a special miracle of deliverance and peace.

Sue gave her life to Jesus Christ in that moment. He gave her peace and strength to move on with her life. In the end, Sue got victory.

Sue opened up to the woman of God about what had happened to her: all the lies, all the cheating, all the hurt, and all the pain. The woman of God shared her testimony with Sue—how her stepdad had raped her as a teenager. But the Lord had given her victory and peace and put His Word in her heart. She could be a mother to her son and daughter. Sue listened to every word.

Three years have passed since then. Sue is working in the women's ministry. God can turn all sadness into joy. The angel of the Lord came by on time that day for Sue. The angel showed her the power of God. Sue was able to go to Kill-Roy and forgive him for all the hurt and pain he had put her through. This also is victory. The Devil doesn't want you to forgive people when they hurt you, but Jesus Christ does. We cannot have true victory until we forgive.

Kill-Roy came to church last Sunday. Saints, let us pray that the Lord will save him. But so many people are still repeating this trend today.

Sue and all her children are saved and working for Jesus Christ. Now this is *victory*! *Victory*! *Victory*! The Devil did not get the victory, and he will not get it in the end.

Thanks for reading my book.

ONE WAY TICKET TO HELL

Sucide the act of Intentionally causing one's own death

Support the gospel of Jesus Christ.

Thinking it's ok

Suicidal behavior is any action that could cause a person to die such as taking a drug overdose, or crashing a car on purpose, or taking a gun an shooting yourself these are all demons spirits that trick your mind JESUS CHRIST LOVES YOU don't be tricked. PLEASE LISTEN no problems, no man, no woman, no job is worth your life these feeling causes you to lose control BUT all these spirits are tricks of the devil he wants to control your mind matthew 26:41 watch and pray that ye enter not into temptation the spirit is indeed is willing, but the flesh is weak. And hearing other people that don't KNOW THE LORD WILL SAY ITS OK BECAUSE THEY DO NOT KNOW THE TRUTH when you die you cannot repent its too late do not be tricked Ecclesiastes chapter 7:16-17 KJV be not righteous over much; neither make thyself over wise: why shouldest thou detroy thyself? Be not over much wicked thou NEITHER be thou FOOLISH; why shouldest thou die before thy TIME? Jeremiah 29:11-12 For I know the thoughts that I think toward you, saith the LORD, thoughts of peace, and not of evil, to give you an expected end. Then shall ye call upon me, and ye shall go and pray unto me, and I will hearken unto you Hebrews10:27 For if we sin willfully after that we have received the knowledge of the truth, there remaineth no more sacrifice for sins. 1 Corinthians 6:19-20 What? Know ye not that your body is the temple of the

Ho'ly ghost which is in you, which ye have of GOD, and ye are not your own? For ye are bought with a price: therefore glorify God in your body, and in your spirit, which are God's. please understand the devil don't want you to hear and take In the truth he's the father of all lies listen to the words of JESUS CHRIST St mark16:16 he that believeth and is baptized shall be saved; but he that believeth not shall be damned. Refuse to go out like that. there was a man in the book of Acts chapter one Now this man purchased a field with the reward of Iniquity and falling headlong,he burst asunder in the midst, and all his bowels gushed out. And it was known unto all the dwellers at Je-ru' sa- lem insomuch as that field is called in their proper tongue, A-cel'da-ma, that is to say the field of blood this is sadness its not ok For it is written in the book of psalms 69:25 Let his habitation be desolate, and let no man dwell therein: And his bishoprick let another take. He lost his place don't lose your place with JESUS CHRIST ju'das hung himself and lost out that he might go to his own place talk to someone tell someone peer pressure influence from members of one's peer group don't allow so called friends or NO ONE cause you to end your life JESUS CHRIST LOVES YOU CALL HIM UP. DON'T BE Intimidated by people, places, or things you can MAKE IT AND NEVER I SAY NEVER GIVE UP.

CALL OUR SPECIAL PRAYER LINE@ 6:46 AM
AND @ 7:00 PM(EST) 1-530-881-1212

CODE 119-540-355

E-MAIL ME ANYTIME
CHARLESGRESHAM61@GMAIL.COM

Printed in the United States
By Bookmasters